BIG-NOTE PIANO

Holiday Fun

ISBN 0-634-04752-3

HAL•LEONARD®
CORPORATION

7777 W. BLUEMOUND RD. P.O. BOX 13819 MILWAUKEE, WI 53213

Visit Hal Leonard Online at
www.halleonard.com

CHRISTMAS TIME IS HERE

from A CHARLIE BROWN CHRISTMAS

Words by LEE MENDELSON
Music by VINCE GUARALDI

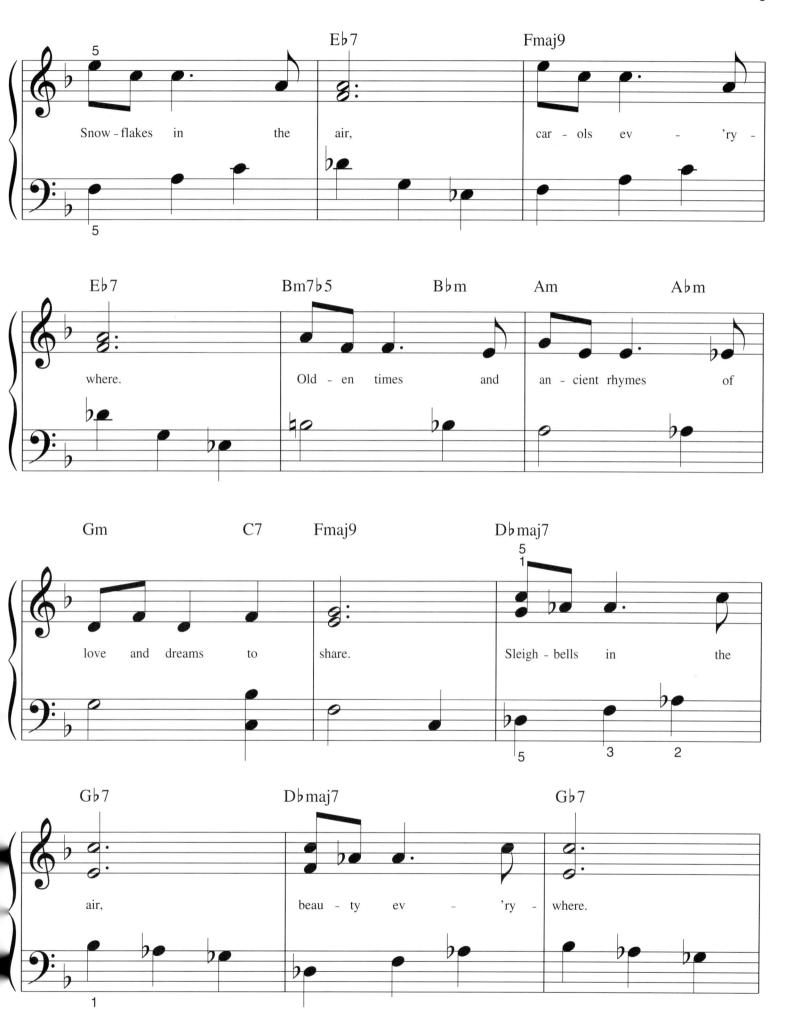

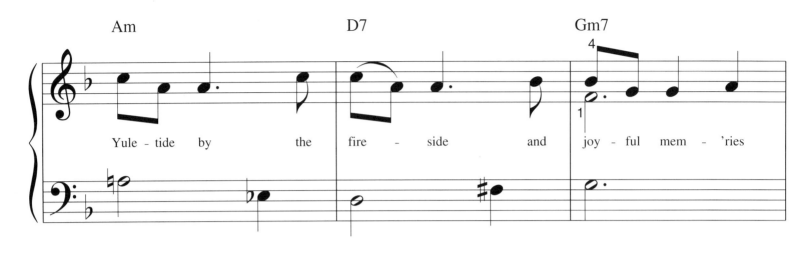

Am — D7 — Gm7

Yule - tide by the fire - side and joy - ful mem - 'ries

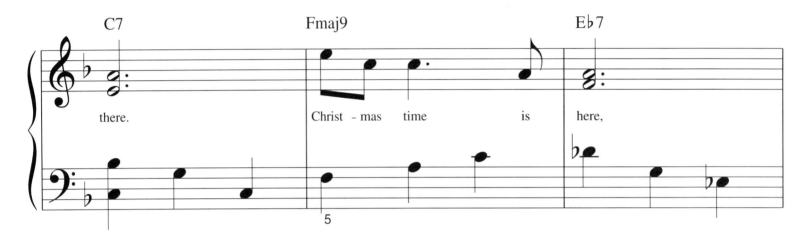

C7 — Fmaj9 — Eb7

there. Christ - mas time is here,

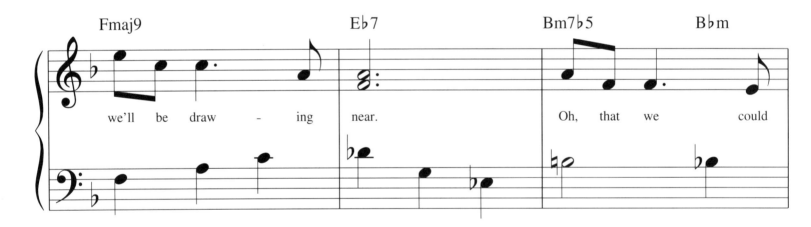

Fmaj9 — Eb7 — Bm7b5 — Bbm

we'll be draw - ing near. Oh, that we could

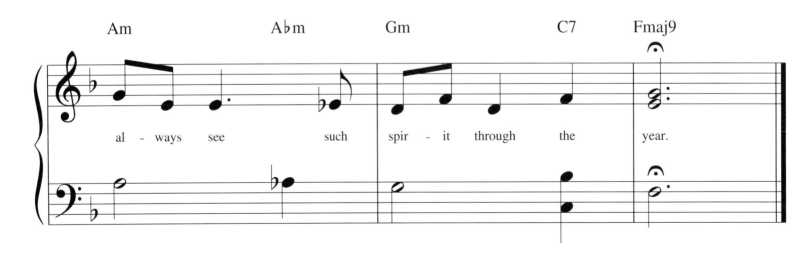

Am — Abm — Gm — C7 — Fmaj9

al - ways see such spir - it through the year.

FELIZ NAVIDAD

Music and Lyrics by
JOSE FELICIANO

Moderately

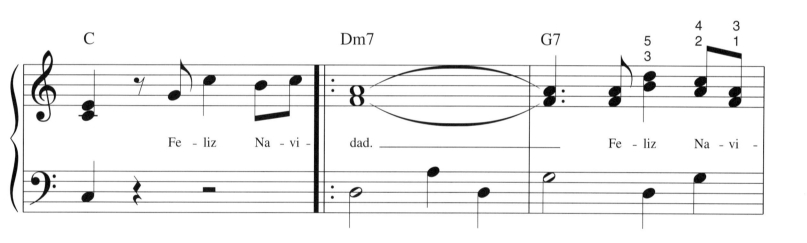

Fe - liz Na - vi - dad. _____ Fe - liz Na - vi -

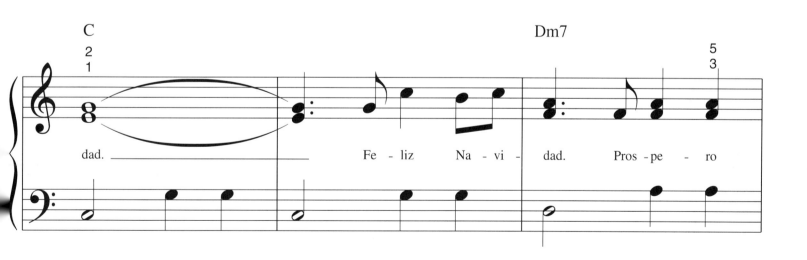

dad. _____ Fe - liz Na - vi - dad. Pros - pe - ro

FROSTY THE SNOW MAN

Words and Music by STEVE NELSON
and JACK ROLLINS

Fros - ty the Snow Man was a jol - ly hap - py
Fros - ty the Snow Man knew the sun was hot that

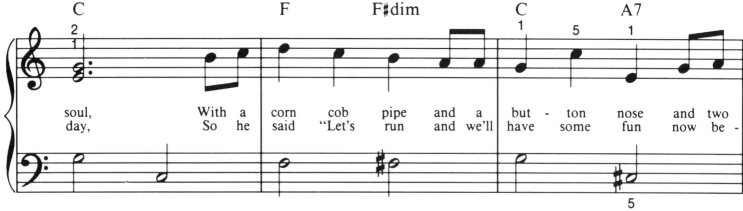

soul, With a corn cob pipe and a but - ton nose and two
day, So he said "Let's run and we'll have some fun now be -

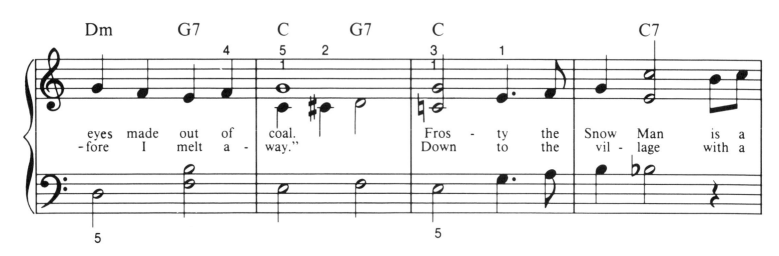

eyes made out of coal. Fros - ty the Snow Man is a
-fore I melt a - way." Down to the vil - lage with a

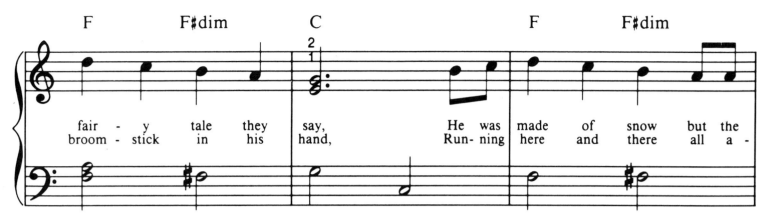

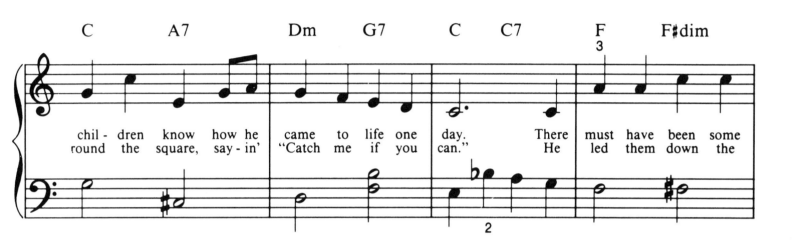

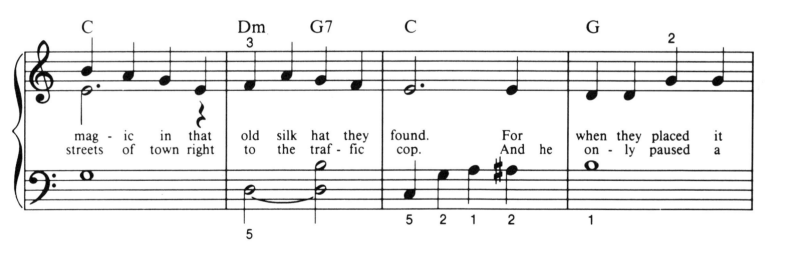

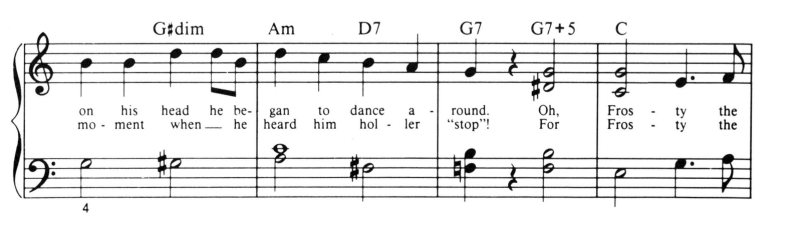

10

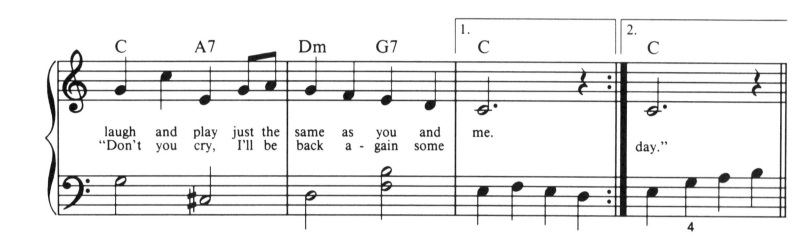

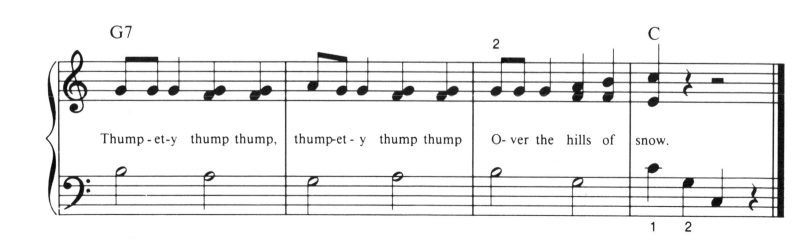

GRANDMA GOT RUN OVER BY A REINDEER

Words and Music by
RANDY BROOKS

12

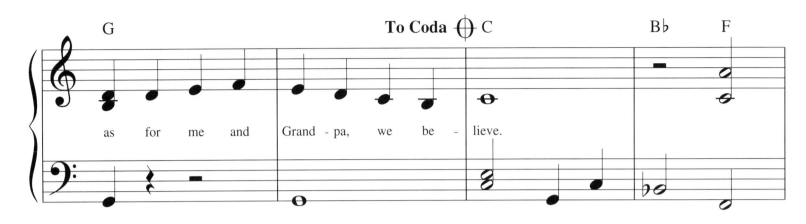

as for me and Grand-pa, we be-lieve.

VERSE:

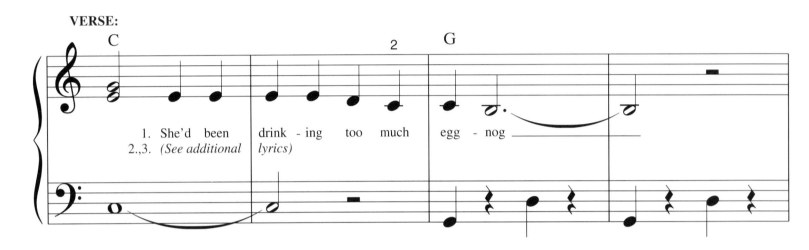

1. She'd been drink-ing too much egg-nog
2.,3. *(See additional lyrics)*

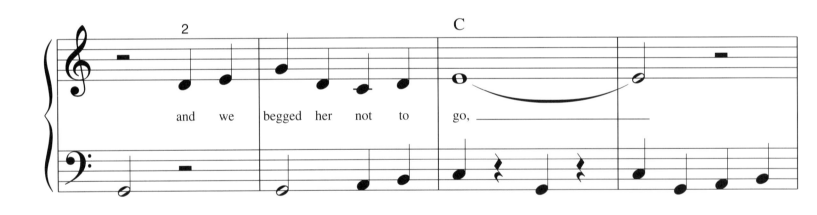

and we begged her not to go,

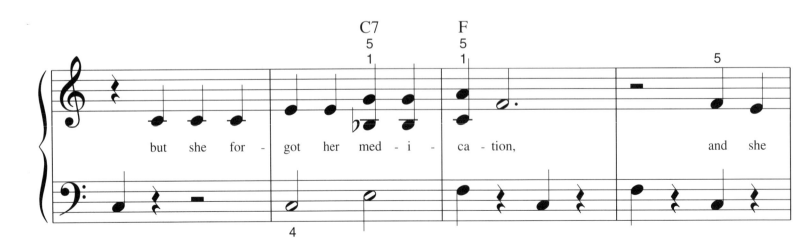

but she for-got her med-i-ca-tion, and she

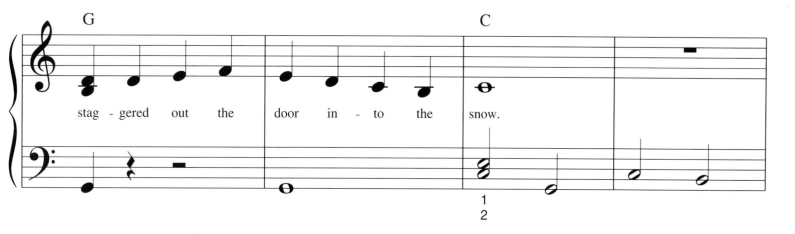

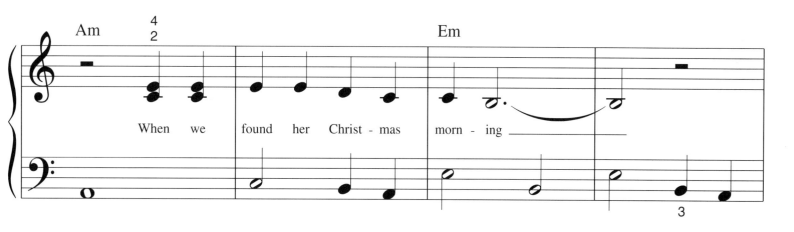

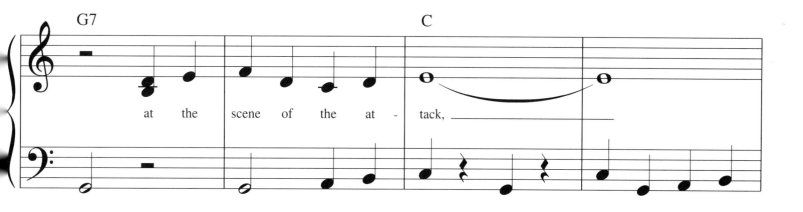

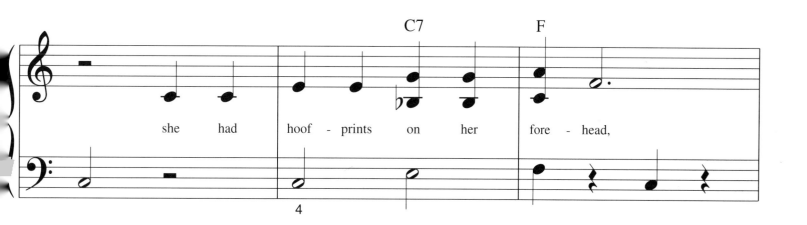

14

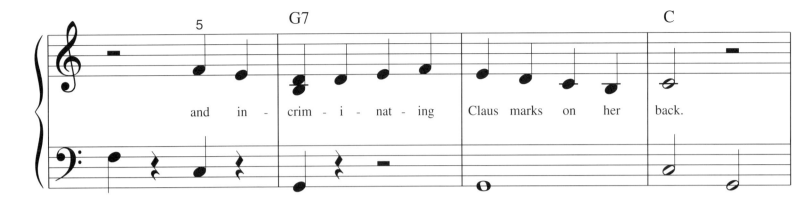

and in - crim - i - nat - ing Claus marks on her back.

1st and 2nd time D.S.
3rd time D.S. al Coda

CODA

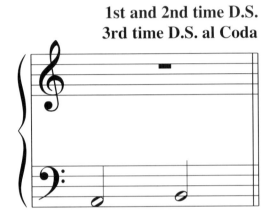

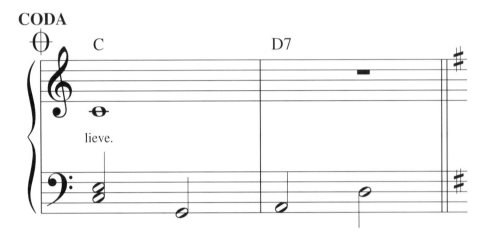

lieve.

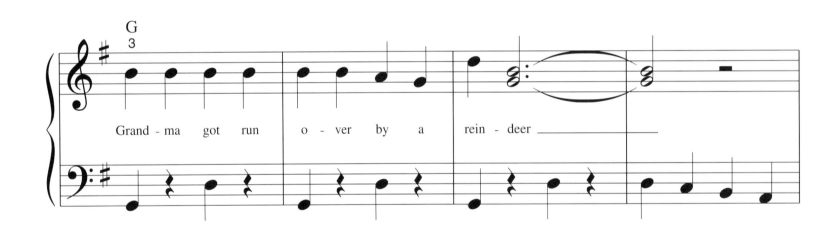

Grand - ma got run o - ver by a rein - deer

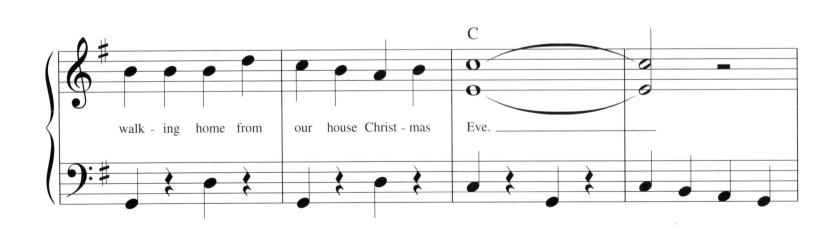

walk - ing home from our house Christ - mas Eve.

Additional Lyrics

2. Now we're all so proud of Grandpa,
   He's been taking this so well.
   See him in there watching football,
   Drinking beer and playing cards with Cousin Mel.
   It's not Christmas without Grandma.
   All the family's dressed in black,
   And we just can't help but wonder:
   Should we open up her gifts or send them back?
   To Chorus

3. Now the goose is on the table,
   And the pudding made of fig,
   And the blue and silver candles,
   That would just have matched the hair in Grandma's wig.
   I've warned all my friends and neighbors,
   Better watch out for yourselves.
   They should never give a license
   To a man who drives a sleigh and plays with elves.
   To Chorus

HAPPY CHRISTMAS, LITTLE FRIEND

Lyrics by OSCAR HAMMERSTEIN II
Music by RICHARD RODGERS

Moderately

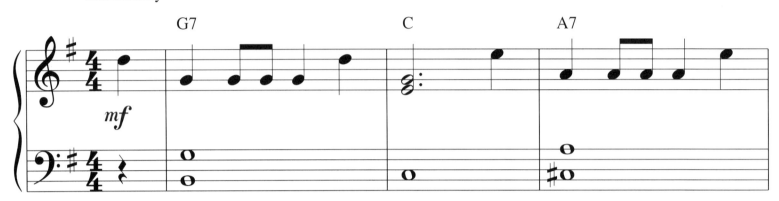

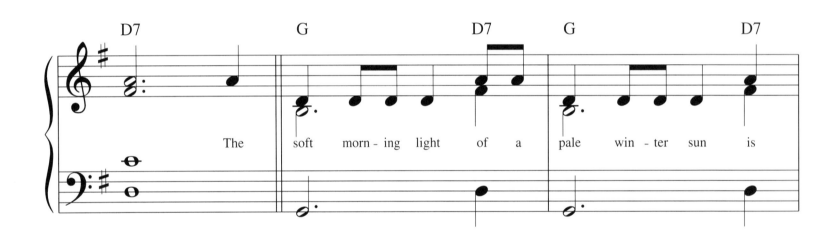

The soft morn - ing light of a pale win - ter sun is

trac - ing the trees on the snow. Leap up lit - tle friend and

HAPPY HOLIDAY
from the Motion Picture Irving Berlin's HOLIDAY INN

Words and Music by
IRVING BERLIN

A HOLLY JOLLY CHRISTMAS

Music and Lyrics by
JOHNNY MARKS

Moderately Bright

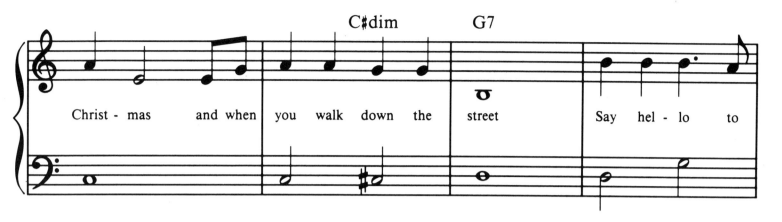

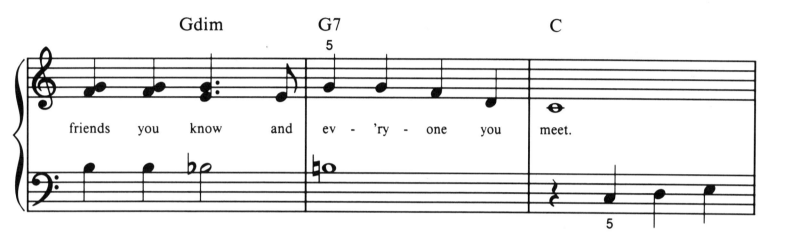

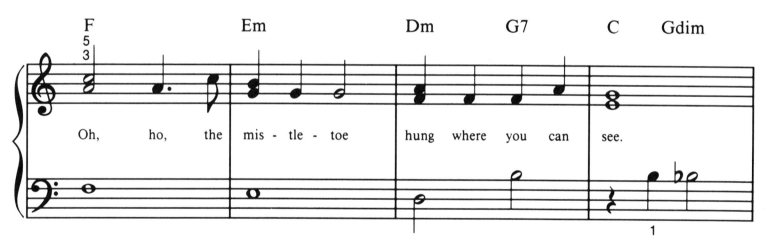

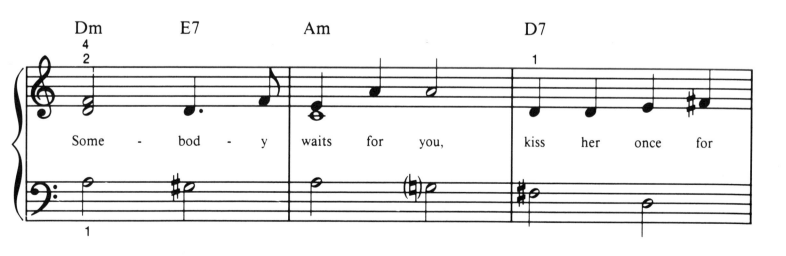

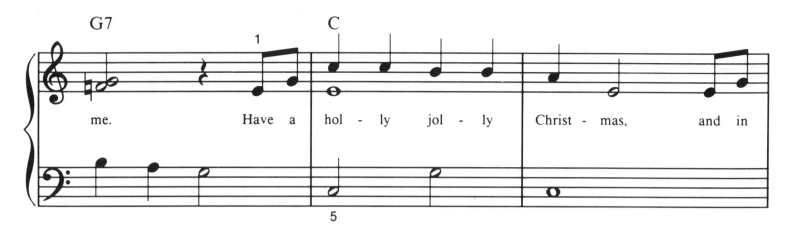

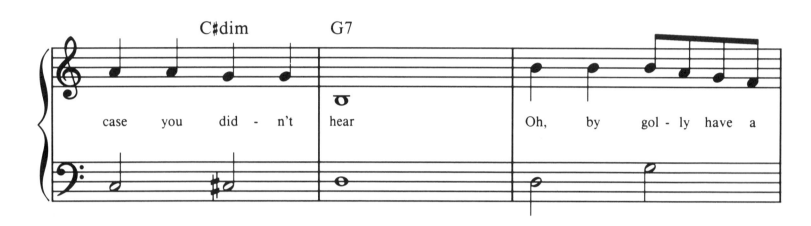

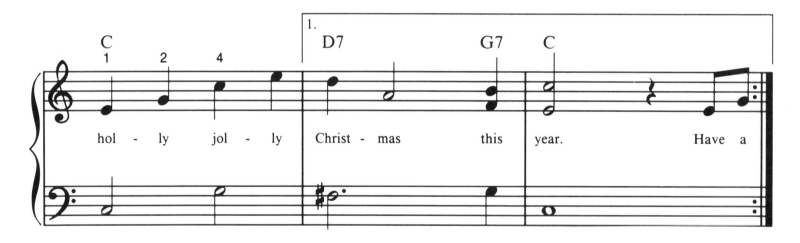

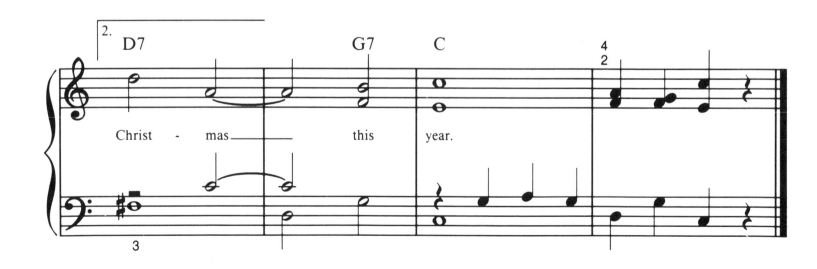

JINGLE-BELL ROCK

Words and Music by JOE BEAL
and JIM BOOTHE

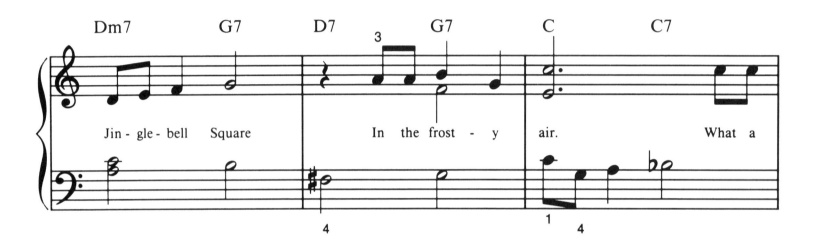

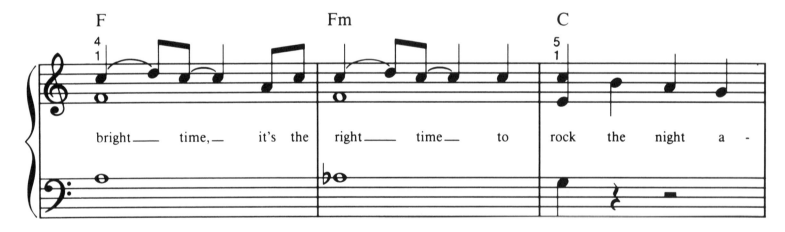

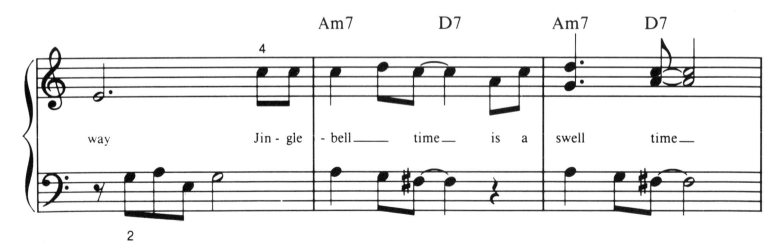

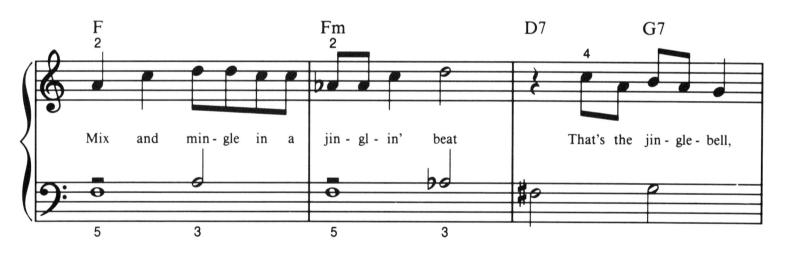

JINGLE, JINGLE, JINGLE

Music and Lyrics by
JOHNNY MARKS

Not too fast

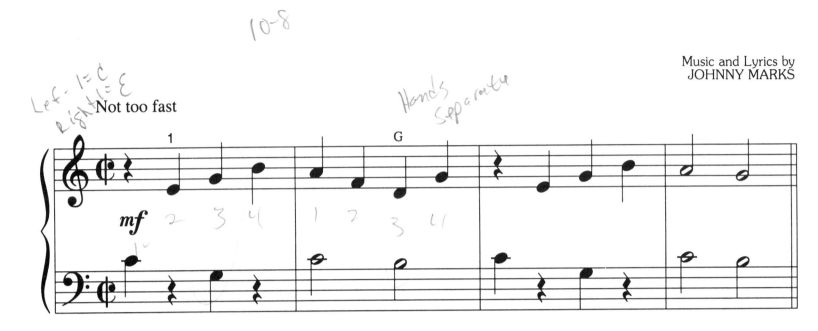

Jin - gle, jin - gle, jin - gle, you will hear {my his} sleigh bells ring.

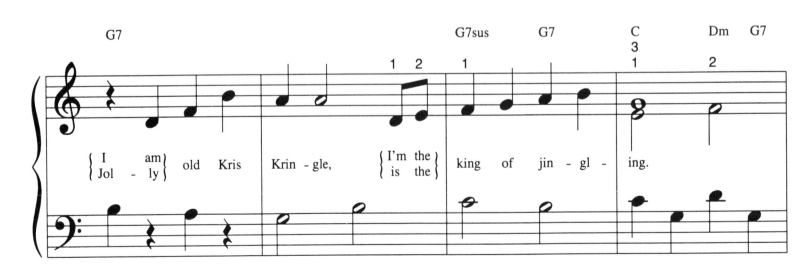

{I am Jol - ly} old Kris Krin - gle, {I'm the is the} king of jin - gl - ing.

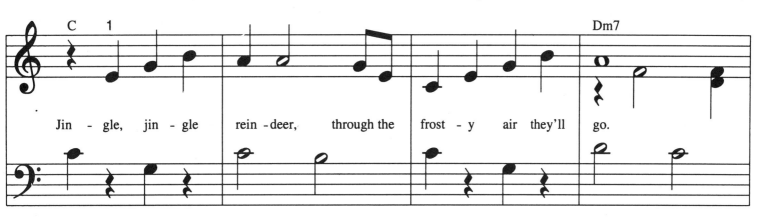

Jin - gle, jin - gle rein - deer, through the frost - y air they'll go.

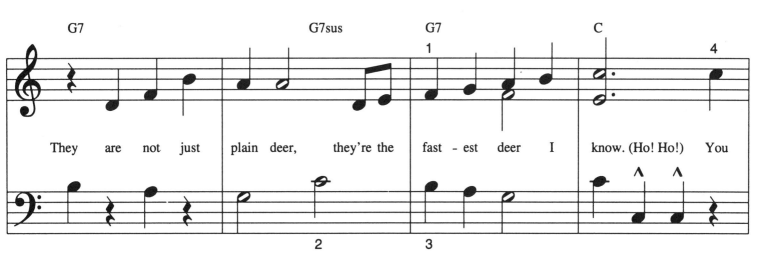

They are not just plain deer, they're the fast - est deer I know. (Ho! Ho!) You

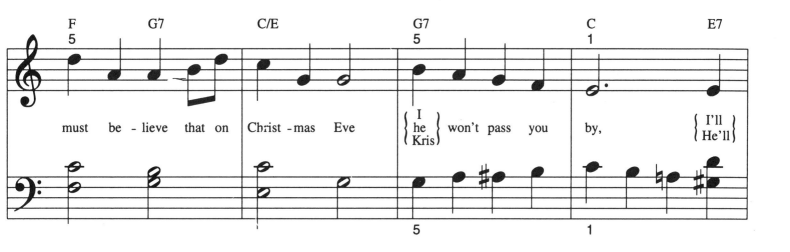

must be - lieve that on Christ -mas Eve {I / he / Kris} won't pass you by, {I'll / He'll}

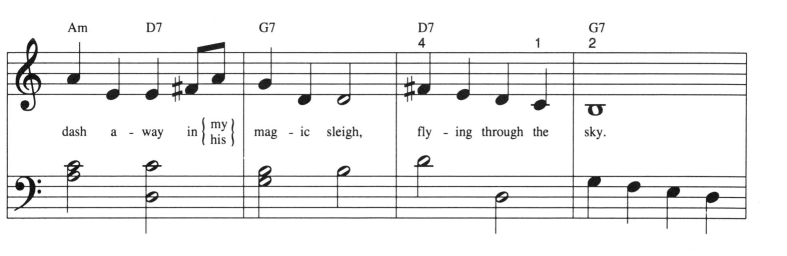

dash a - way in {my / his} mag - ic sleigh, fly - ing through the sky.

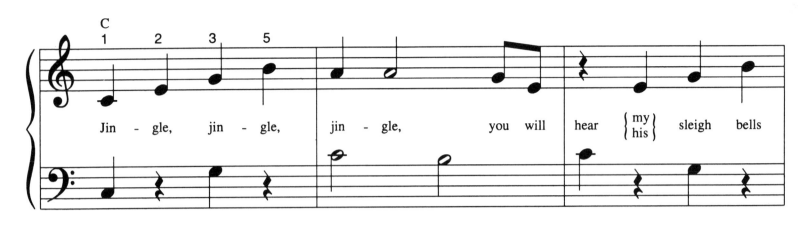

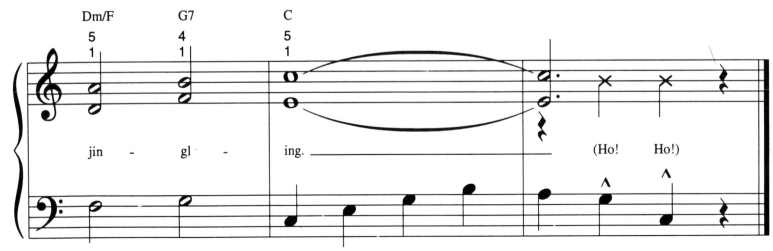

ROCKIN' AROUND THE CHRISTMAS TREE

Music and Lyrics by
JOHNNY MARKS

34

MERRY CHRISTMAS, DARLING

Words and Music by RICHARD CARPENTER
and FRANK POOLER

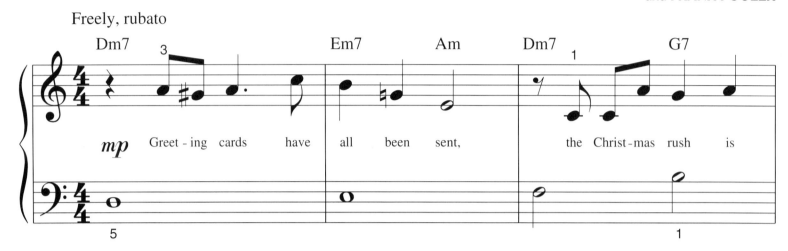

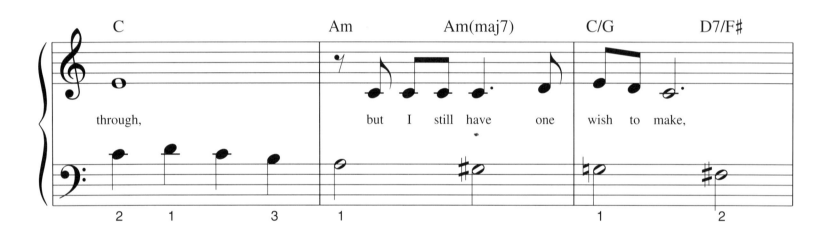

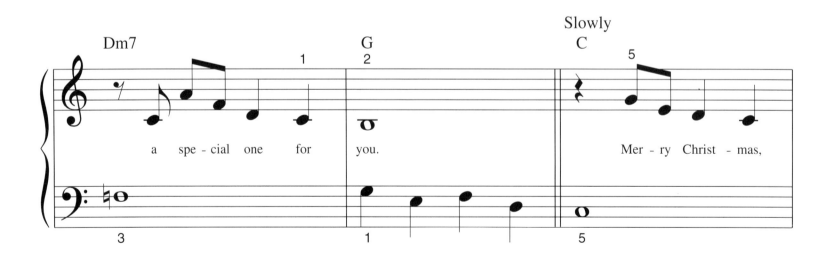

38

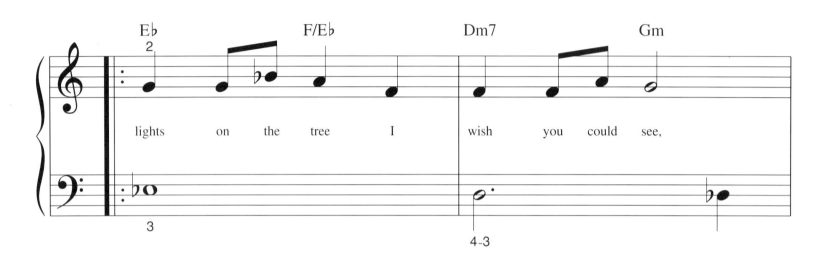

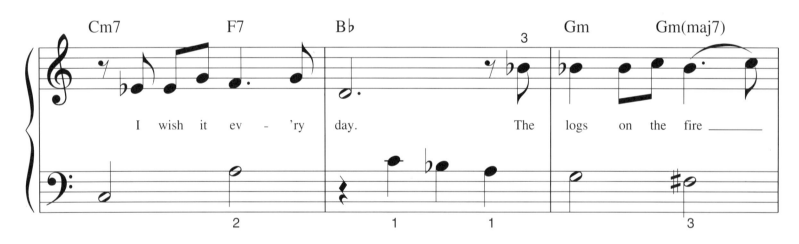

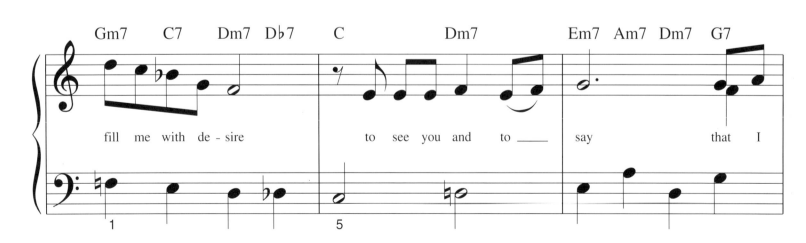

THE MERRY CHRISTMAS POLKA

Words by PAUL FRANCIS WEBSTER
Music by SONNY BURKE

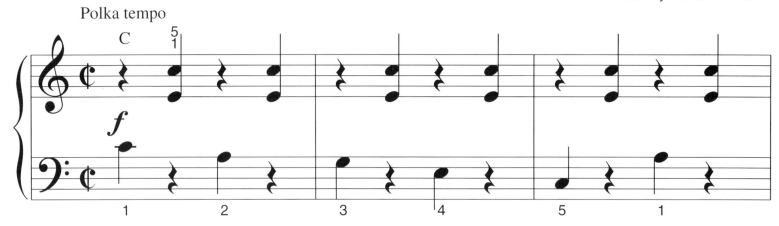

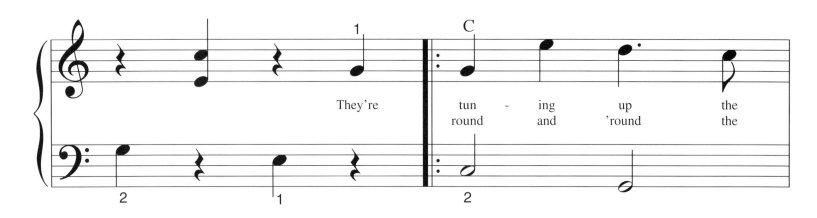

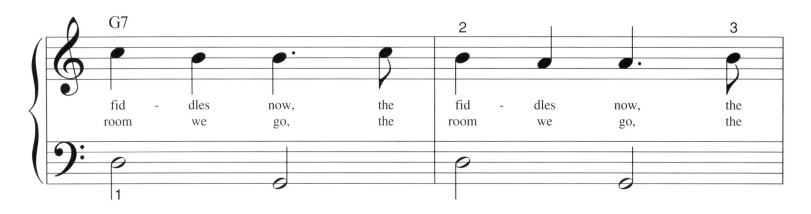

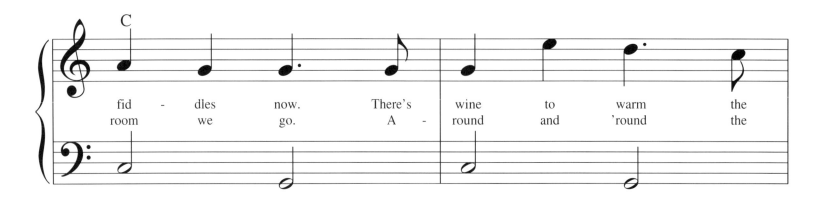

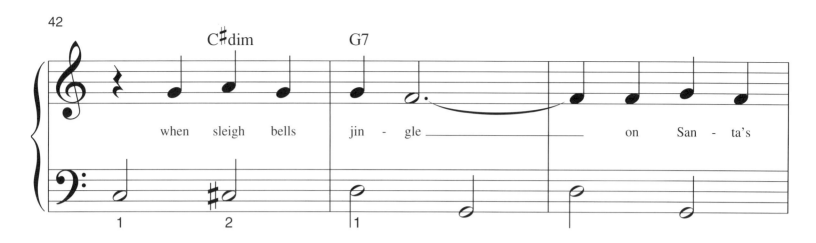

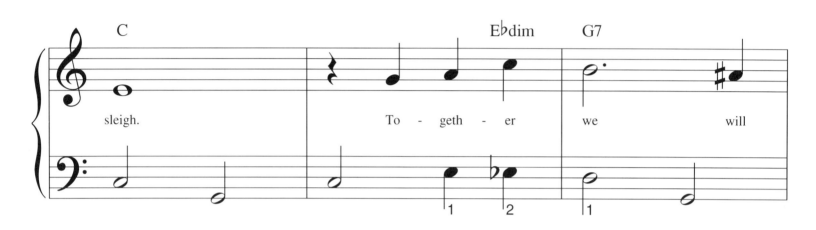

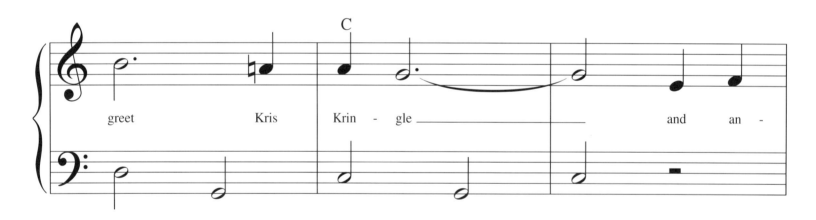

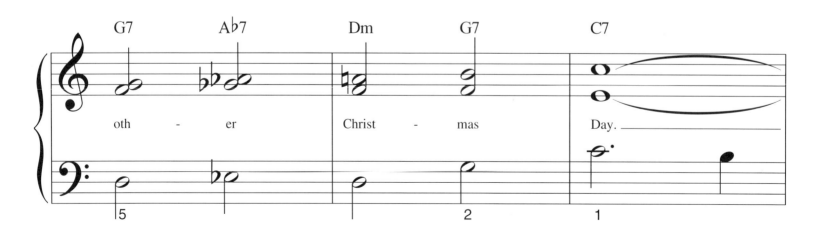

Come on and

dance   The   Mer - ry   Christ - mas   Pol - ka.

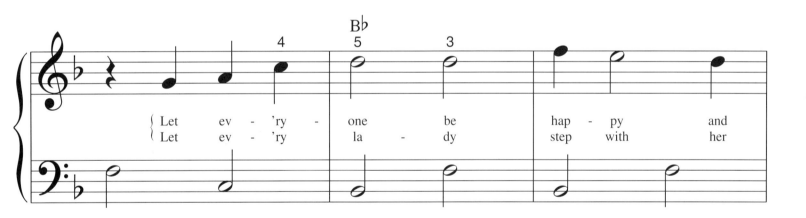

Let   ev - 'ry - one   be   hap - py   and
Let   ev - 'ry   la - dy   step   with   her

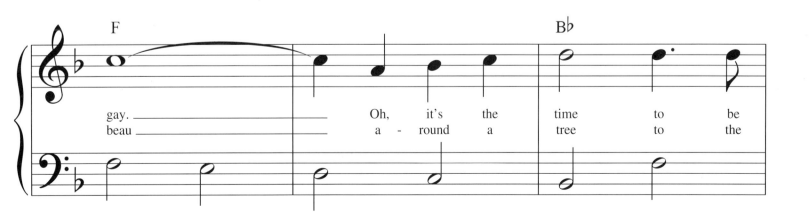

gay. _____   Oh,   it's   the   time   to   be
beau _____   a - round   a   tree   to   the

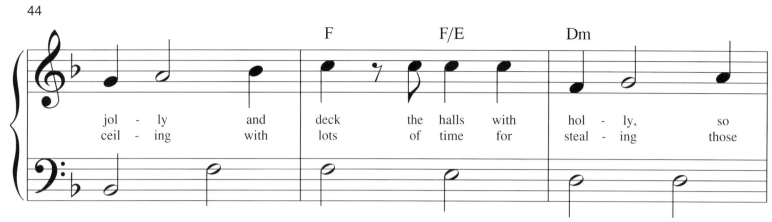

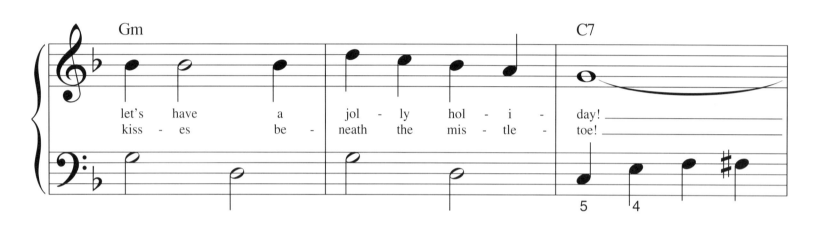

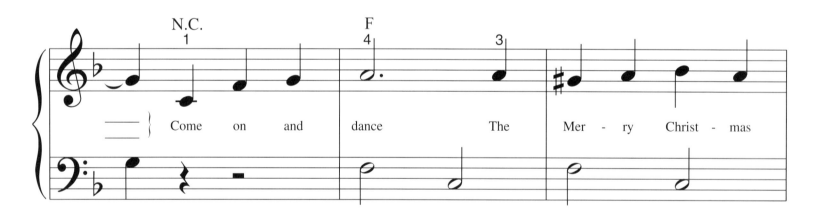

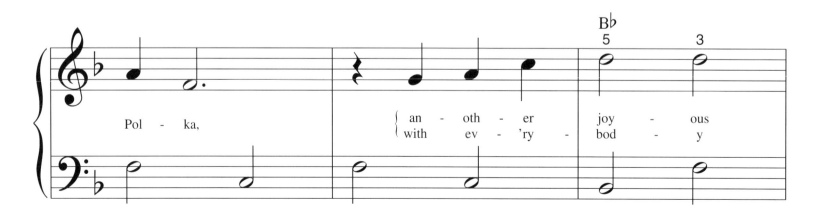

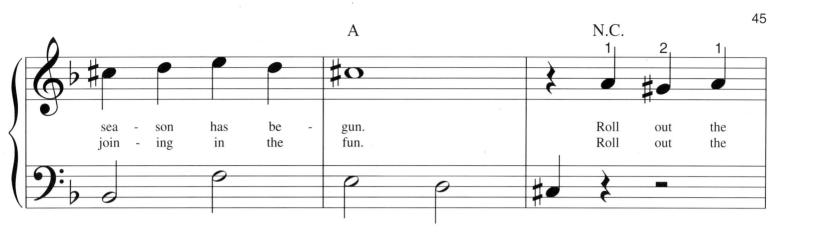

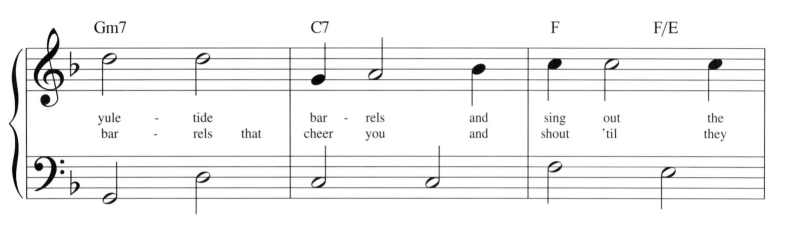

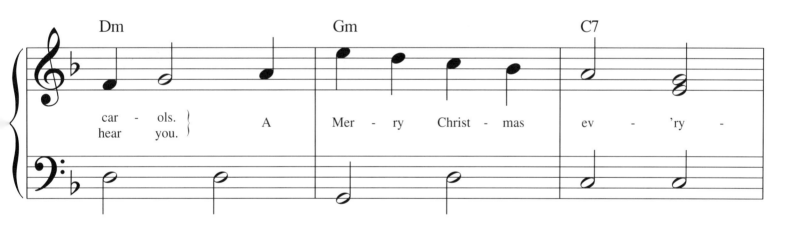

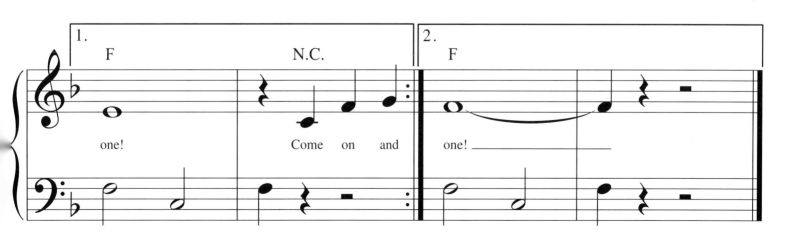

MISTER SANTA

Words and Music by
PAT BALLARD

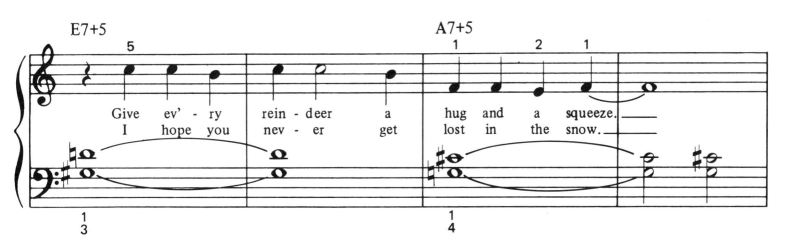

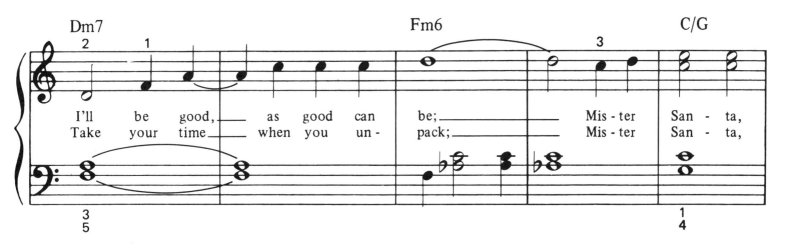

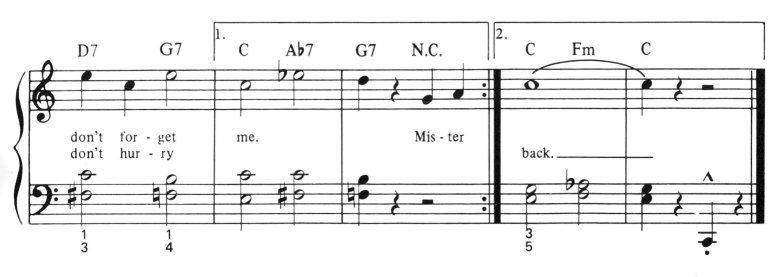

RUDOLPH THE RED-NOSED REINDEER

Music and Lyrics by
JOHNNY MARKS

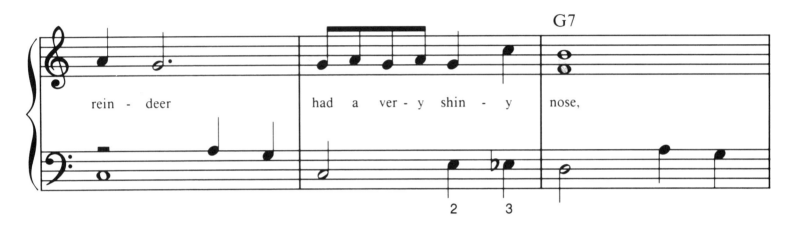

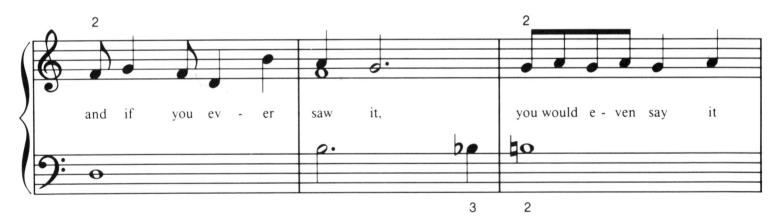

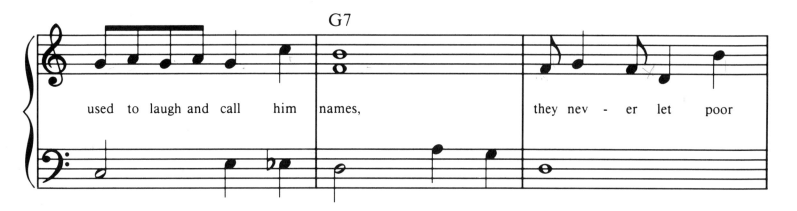

used to laugh and call   him   names,   they   nev - er   let   poor

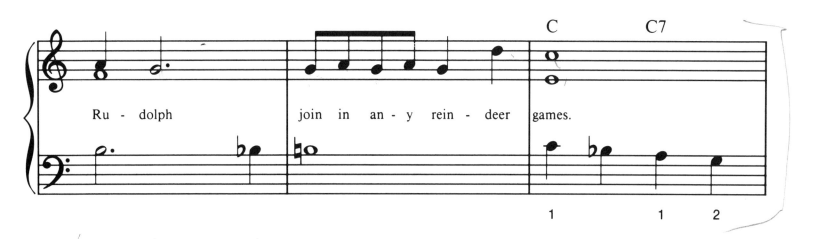

Ru - dolph   join in an - y rein - deer games.

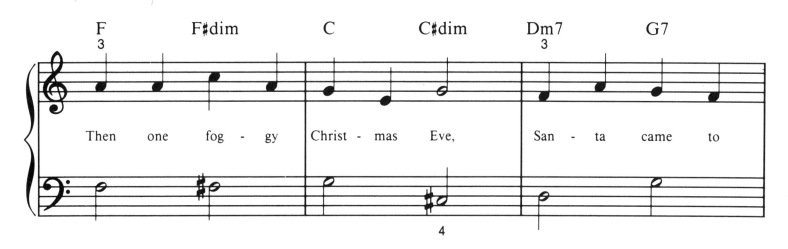

Then   one   fog - gy   Christ - mas Eve,   San - ta   came to

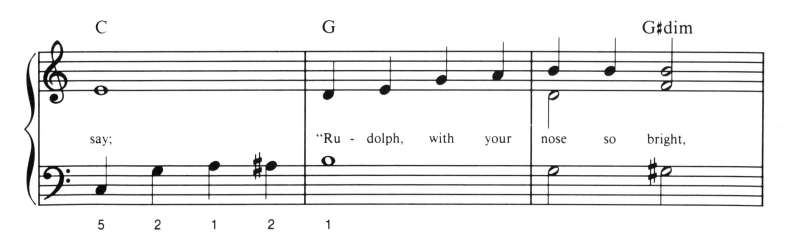

say;   "Ru - dolph, with   your   nose   so   bright,

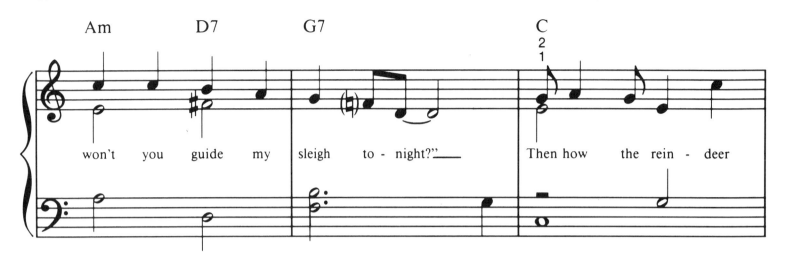

Am   D7   G7   C

won't you guide my sleigh to-night?"____ Then how the rein - deer

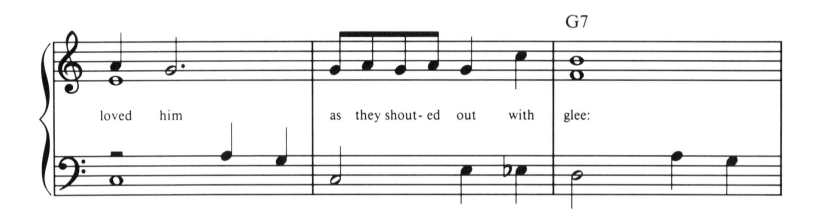

G7

loved him   as they shout-ed out with   glee:

Gdim

"Ru-dolph, the red - nosed rein - deer,   You'll go down in

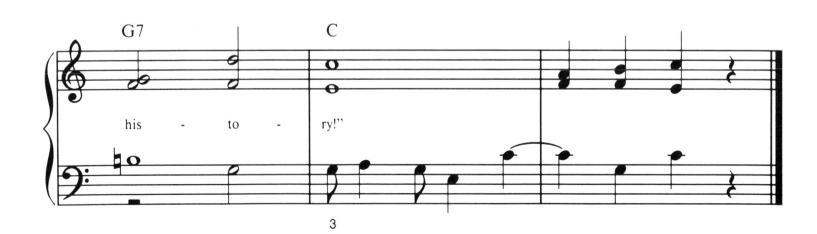

G7   C

his - to - ry!"

3

SANTA, BRING MY BABY BACK
(To Me)

Words and Music by CLAUDE DeMETRUIS
and AARON SCHROEDER

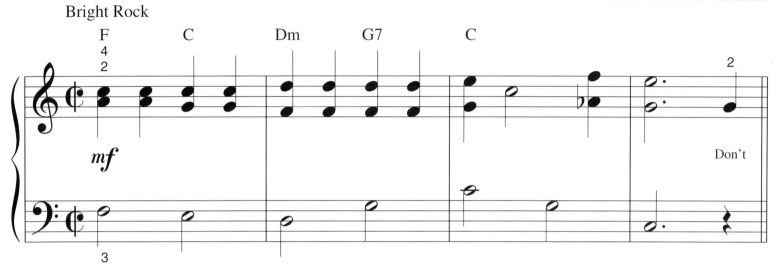

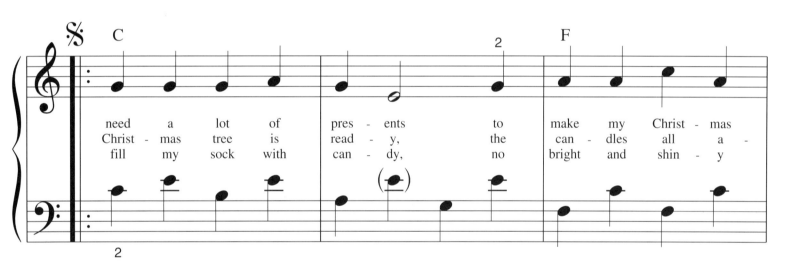

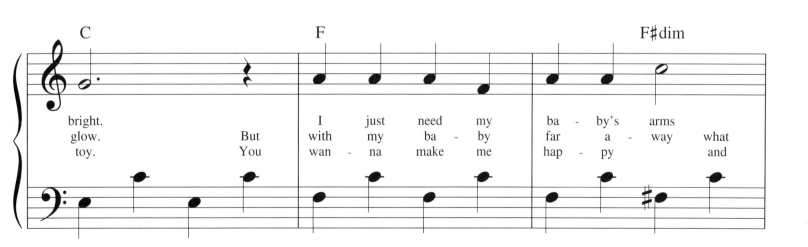

SANTA BABY

By JOAN JAVITS, PHIL SPRINGER
and TONY SPRINGER

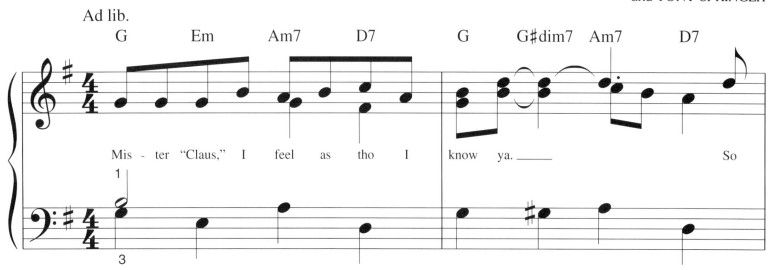

Mis- ter "Claus," I feel as tho I know ya. _____ So

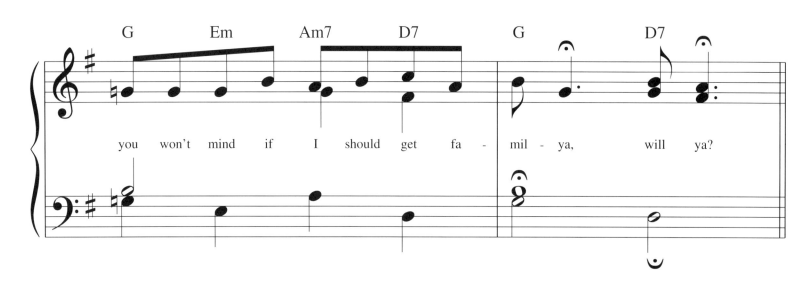

you won't mind if I should get fa - mil - ya, will ya?

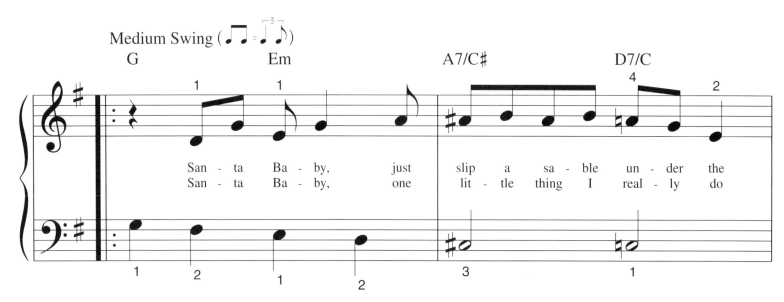

San - ta Ba - by, just slip a sa - ble un - der the
San - ta Ba - by, one lit - tle thing I real - ly do

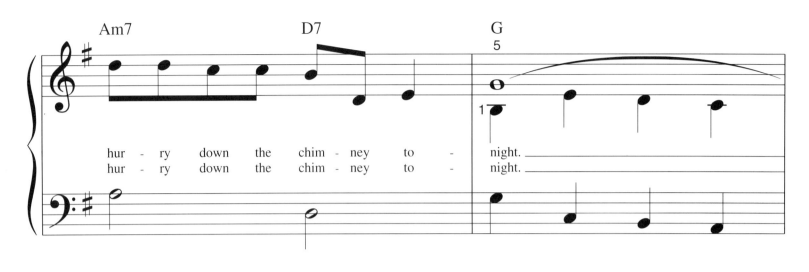

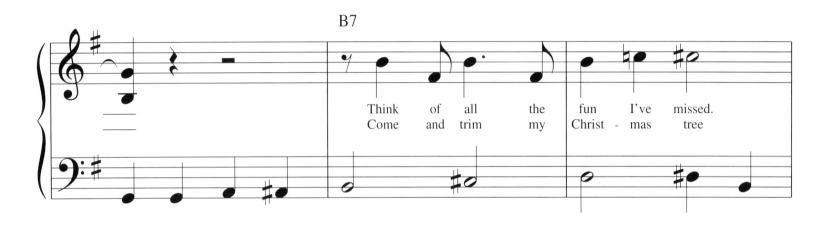

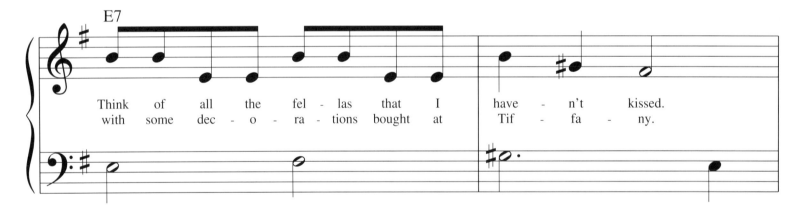

SANTA CLAUS IS BACK IN TOWN

Words and Music by JERRY LEIBER
and MIKE STOLLER

Christ - mas time, pret - ty ba - by, and the snow is fall - in' on the ground. ___

You be a

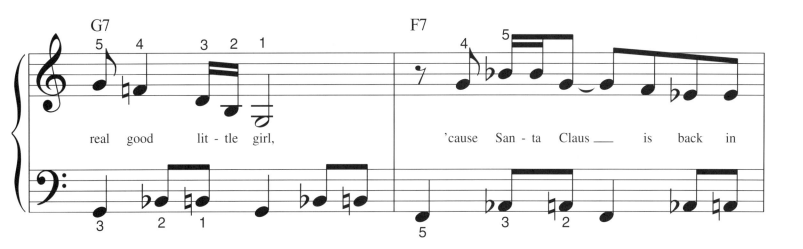

real good lit - tle girl, 'cause San - ta Claus ___ is back in

town.

60

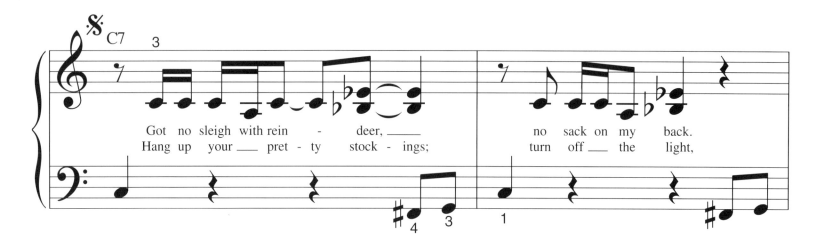

Got no sleigh with rein - deer, _____ no sack on my back.
Hang up your ___ pret - ty stock - ings; turn off ___ the light,

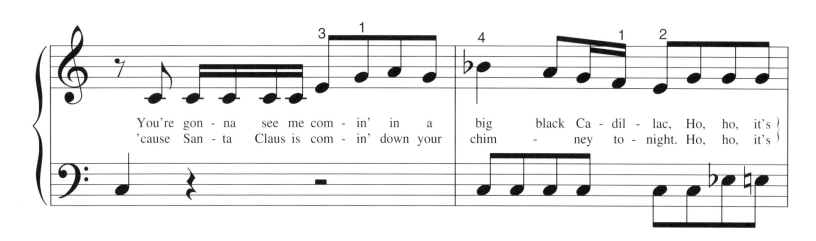

You're gon - na see me com - in' in a big black Ca - dil - lac, Ho, ho, it's
'cause San - ta Claus is com - in' down your chim - ney to - night. Ho, ho, it's

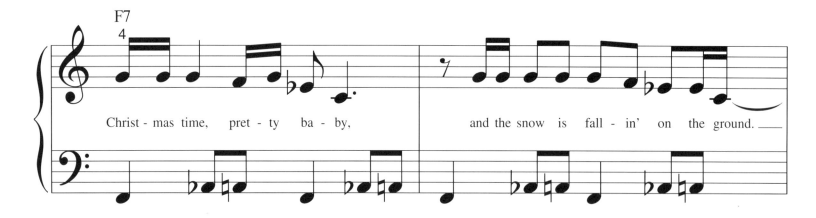

Christ - mas time, pret - ty ba - by, and the snow is fall - in' on the ground. ___

You be a

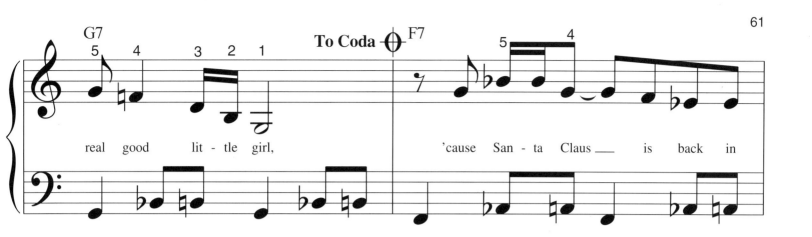

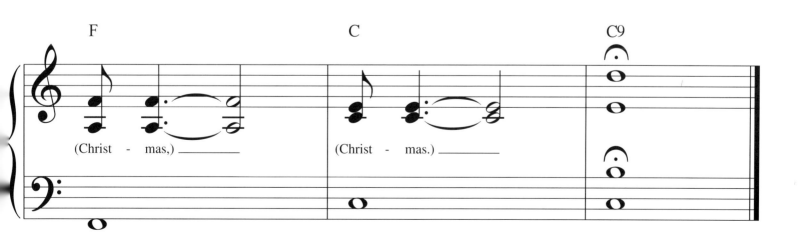

SHAKE ME I RATTLE
(Squeeze Me I Cry)

Moderately slow

Words and Music by HAL HACKADY
and CHARLES NAYLOR

pass - ing by a toy shop on the cor - ner of the
called an - oth - er toy shop on a square so long a-

Square, where a lit - tle girl was look - ing
go Where I saw a lit - tle dol - ly

SUZY SNOWFLAKE

Words and Music by SID TEPPER
and ROY BENNETT

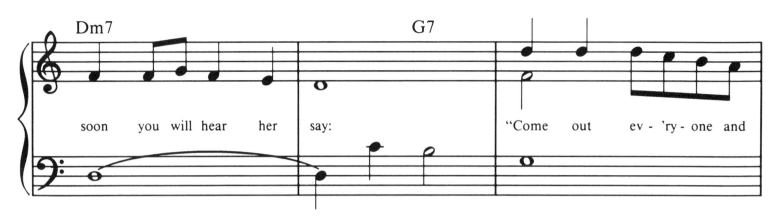

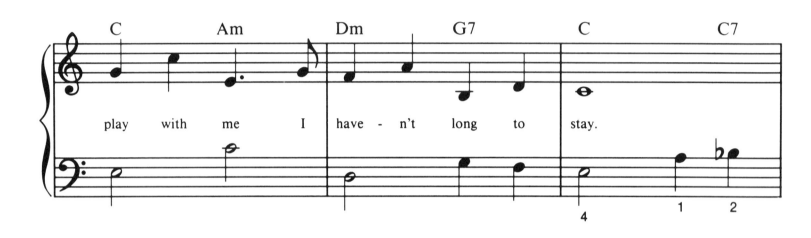

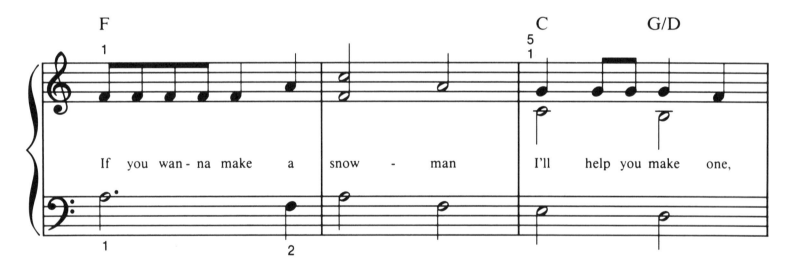

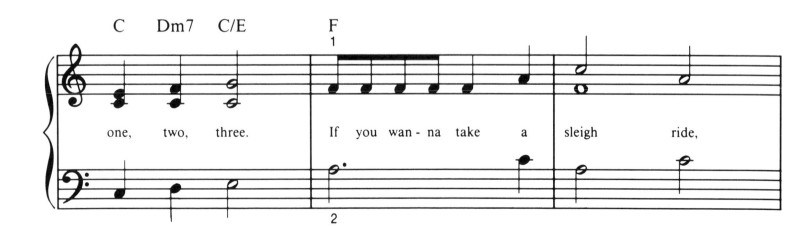

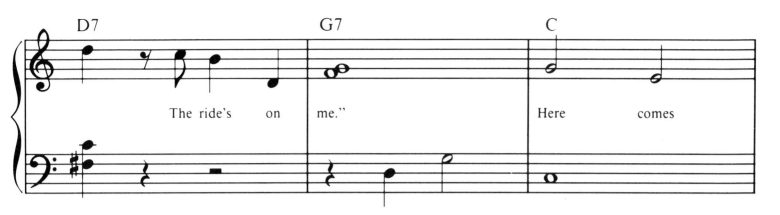

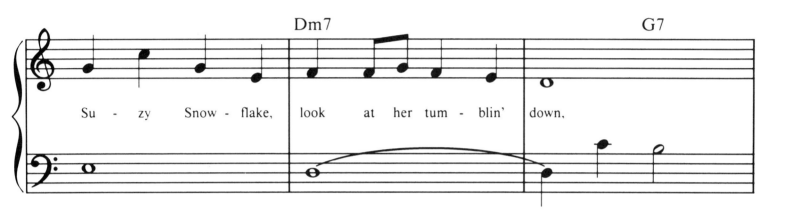

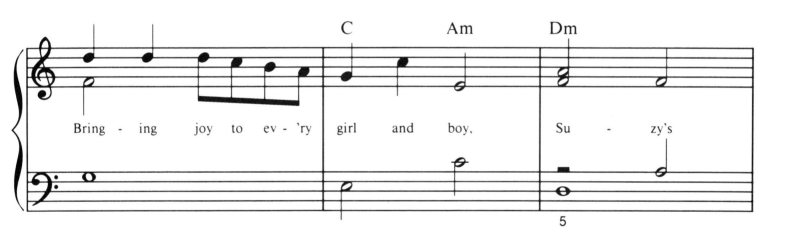

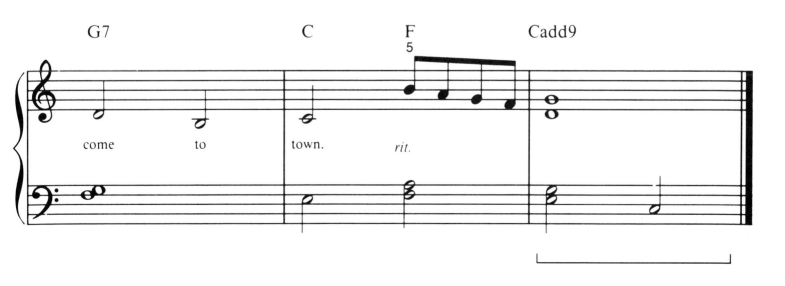

WONDERFUL CHRISTMASTIME

Words and Music by
McCARTNEY

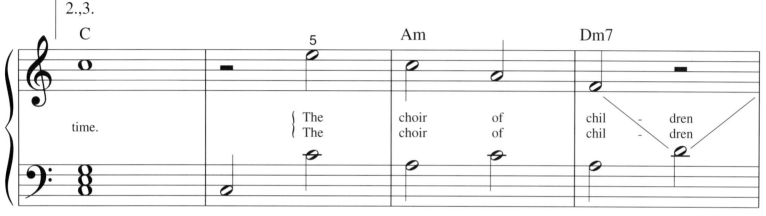

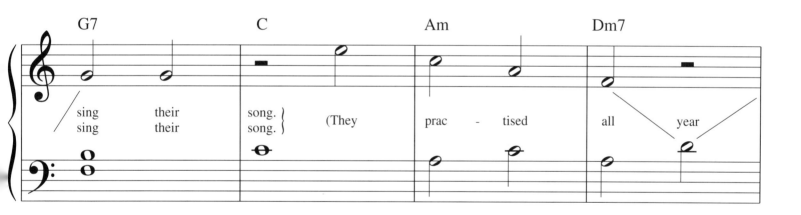

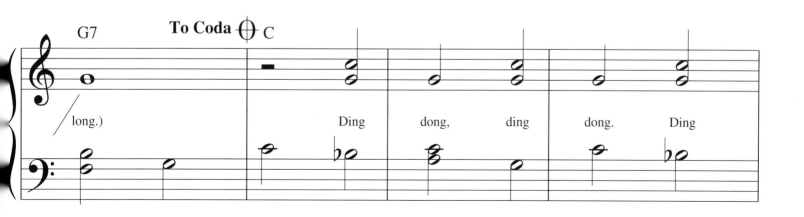

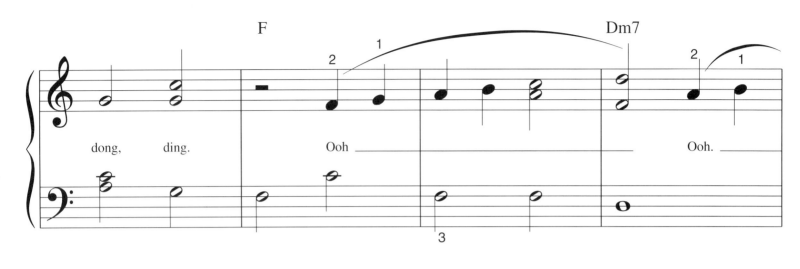

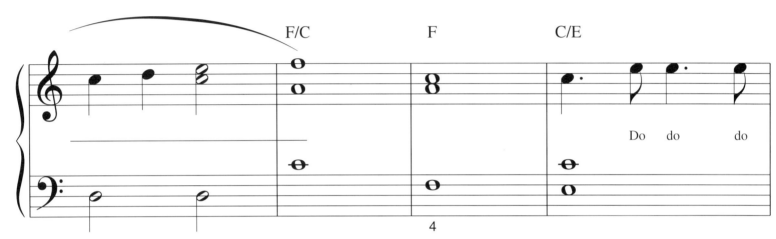

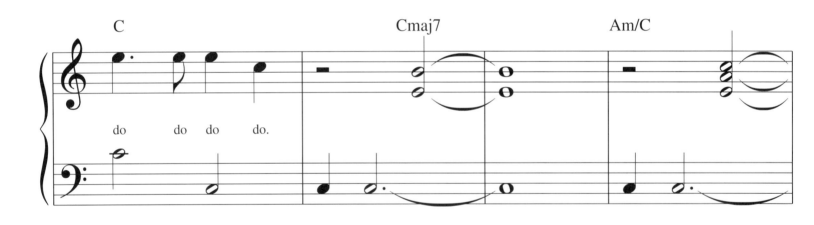

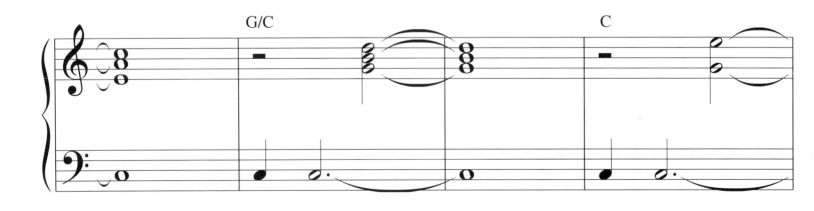

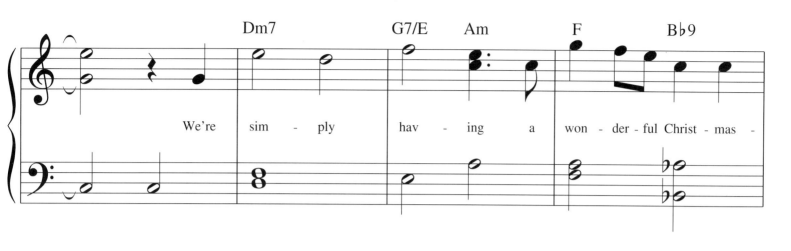

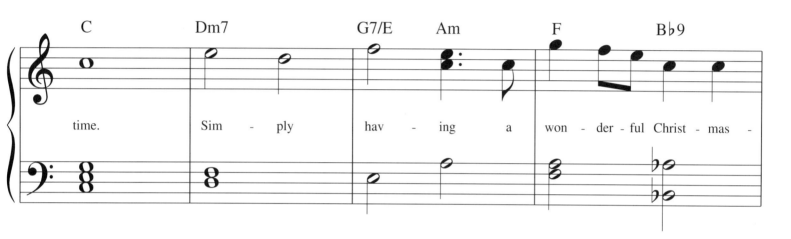

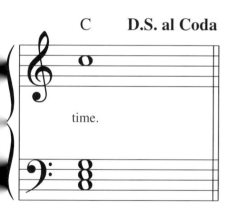

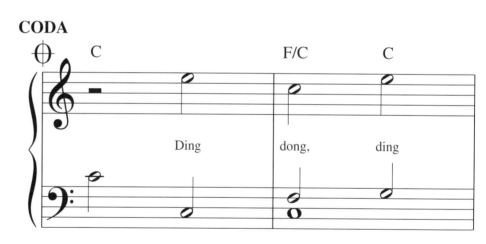

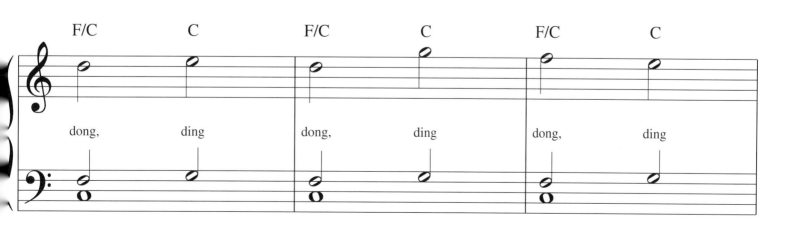

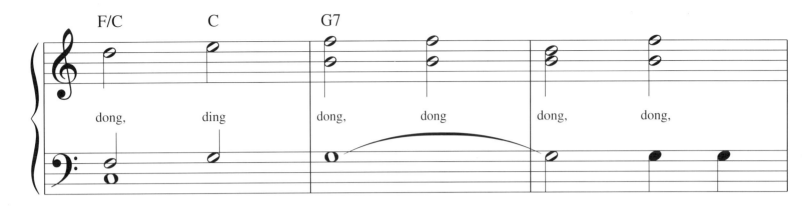

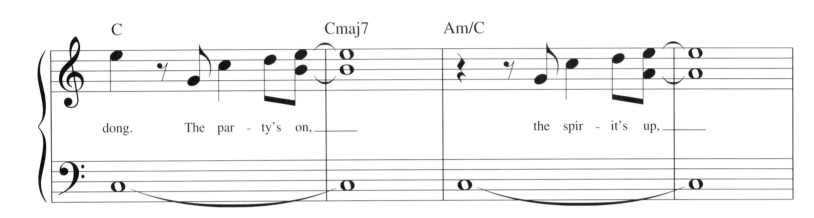

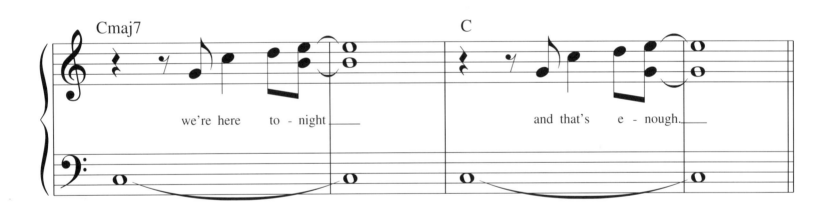